T0413343

SURVIVING THE BLITZ OF WORLD WAR II

A HISTORY-SEEKING ADVENTURE

by Allison Lassieur

CAPSTONE PRESS
a capstone imprint

Published by Capstone Press, an imprint of Capstone
1710 Roe Crest Drive, North Mankato, Minnesota 56003
capstonepub.com

Library of Congress Cataloging-in-Publication Data is available on the Library of
Congress website.
ISBN: 9781669083467 (hardcover)
ISBN: 9781669083436 (paperback)
ISBN: 9781669083443 (ebook PDF)

Summary: YOU are a British citizen during World War II when the German
Blitzkrieg—or Blitz—begins. Night after night, waves of German planes drop
hundreds of bombs on cities and towns all over Great Britain. How will you protect
yourself during these terrifying attacks? What will you do to help your neighbors
and community survive? Step back in time to face the dangers and difficult
decisions real people encountered during the Blitz of World War II.

Editorial Credits
Editors: Alison Deering and Christopher Harbo; Designer: Bobbie Nuytten;
Media Researcher: Svetlana Zhurkin; Production Specialist: Whitney Schaefer

Image Credits
Alamy: Chronicle, 14; Getty Images: Central Press, 56, 69, Fox Photos, 88, 93,
Fox Photos/George W. Hales, 81, Fox Photos/M. McNeill, 28, Fox Photos/
William Vanderson, 4, Hulton Archive/Fox Photos, 8, 46, 104, Hulton Archive/
Fox Photos/George W. Hales, 85, Hulton Archive/Fox Photos/Reg Speller, 103,
Hulton Archive/Picture Post/Bert Hardy, 31, Imperial War Museums/Ministry of
Information Photo Division Photographer, 76, Keystone, 53, 95, Mirrorpix/Daily
Mirror/Edward Dean, 62, Topical Press Agency/Davis, 100, Topical Press Agency/
H.F. Davis, cover; Newscom: Everett Collection, 60, Mirrorpix, 21

Printed and bound in China. PO 6097

TABLE OF CONTENTS

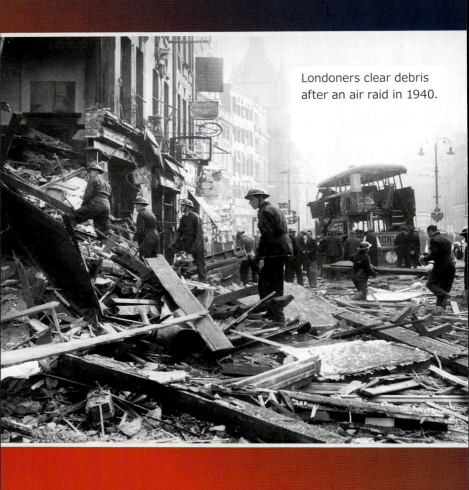

Londoners clear debris after an air raid in 1940.

ABOUT YOUR ADVENTURE

YOU are a loyal British subject during World War II (1939–1945), and the threat of war with Nazi Germany hangs over the whole country. People say the German Nazi leader, Adolf Hitler, has ordered attacks on England.

You could be living in London when the first bombs fall. Or you may be helping your neighbors dodge German bombs in Liverpool. You could be in Coventry, fighting deadly fires from bombs exploding all around. Wherever you are, YOU CHOOSE which path to take. Will you live through another night of attacks? Or, will you perish during the next bombing run?

Turn the page to begin your adventure.

CHAPTER 1

FIRE FROM THE SKY

Saturday, September 7, 1940, started out as a beautiful day in England. Then out of nowhere, waves of German bombers appeared in the sky. For hours, they dropped hundreds of bombs on the city of London. By the time the attack was over, 430 people were dead. More than a thousand had been injured. This day, now known as Black Saturday, was the first day of the Blitz.

The Blitz—short for *Blitzkrieg*, which means "lightning war" in German—was a series of deadly aerial attacks on Great Britain by the Luftwaffe, Adolf Hitler's Air Force. World War II had been raging since 1939, a year before the Blitz began. Hitler had already conquered many European countries. Great Britain's prime minister, Winston

Turn the page.

Churchill, knew Hitler would come for Great Britain next—and he was right.

For eight months, the Luftwaffe carried out deadly and terrifying night attacks on cities and towns all over Great Britain. But the British people were ready. Many women and children were evacuated to the countryside. Air raid shelters were built around the country. Every town had trained Air Raid Precaution (ARP) wardens

ARP wardens on a rooftop scan the sky for German bombers in 1940.

to watch for bombers, help the injured, and guide people to safety during an attack. They also had volunteer firemen to put out blazes. These preparations helped save thousands of people.

Finally, Hitler realized that Great Britain would not be broken. He ordered the Luftwaffe to end the attacks. Great Britain had beaten Hitler and the Nazis but at a terrible cost. Millions of people were dead, injured, or homeless. Destruction was everywhere. But the British people had bravely stood up to Hitler and the Luftwaffe.

Would you be brave enough to face the dangers of the Blitz? Could you dodge bombs, help the injured, and face the possibility of death every day?

- To experience the Blitz as a twelve-year-old in London, turn to page 11.
- To be an ARP warden in Liverpool, turn to page 41.
- To face the Blitz as a firefighter in Coventry, turn to page 75.

CHAPTER 2

KEEPING CALM AND CARRYING ON

It's 1940, and life in the big city of London is all you've ever known. You live with your mother, father, and baby brother, George, in a small, cozy house. Every day, Papa goes to work. Mama stays home with George while you go to school a few blocks away.

You know about the war in Europe. But Europe is far away. You don't think it will ever touch you. Then one day, bombs start falling out of the sky. Papa explains that Adolf Hitler, the leader of Nazi Germany, wants to conquer Great Britain and has ordered the Luftwaffe to attack London and other British towns and

Turn the page.

cities. Hitler hopes that the attacks will force the British people to surrender to German forces.

Soon, the attacks become a way of life. Every night, the roar of the Luftwaffe's engines fills the air. Bombs fall, and explosions shake the earth. Huge fires turn the sky red and orange. The Luftwaffe's targets are mainly docks, airports, and factories that manufacture goods and weapons. Hundreds of people who live near these places die each night. Thousands more are injured or left homeless.

Each morning, Londoners wake up to damaged and destroyed buildings and houses. But they carry on as best as they can. People go to work or school. Cleanup crews clear rubble from the streets. You try to act normal, too, but fear knots your stomach each afternoon as the sun begins to set. That's when the sirens wail, warning of a new attack.

So far, the Luftwaffe's targets are areas far away from your neighborhood. Papa says it's because they want to destroy British ships and airplanes, not homes. But lately, the bombs have been getting closer. Mama and Papa talk about what to do. One idea is to go stay with your Aunt Gracie, Mama's sister, in Canada. But Canada is very far away and there's not enough money to get there. So, your family must stay in London for now.

Papa wants to build an Anderson shelter—a small structure that holds only a few people—in your back garden. Mama wants to go to a public shelter, like a school basement or a London Underground station—the city's version of a subway. Hundreds of people go to those places every night when an attack comes.

- If you want Papa to build an Anderson shelter, turn to page 14.
- If you think a public shelter is safer, turn to page 27.

Papa comes home with a truckload of lumber, sheet metal, and other supplies. He and other neighbors dig a deep hole in the back garden. The men build the shelter in the hole, carefully putting together sheet metal walls and a curved roof. Then they pile dirt all around it. Burying the shelter underground makes it safer from bombs and shrapnel.

Two men build an Anderson shelter for protection from German air raids.

After the shelter is finished, Mama carries food, bedding, and other items inside. The Anderson shelter is just for bombing emergencies, and the attacks only last through the night. You'll probably have to sleep in the shelter sometimes, and Mama wants to be prepared.

When the sirens start that evening, you all hurry into the shelter. It's tiny and dark, and it smells like wet dirt.

Before long, George starts crying. He wants Mr. Booboo, his toy rabbit. You could run into the house to get his toy. Surely it would be safe to leave the shelter for a few minutes. Or, you could stay in the shelter and hope George calms down on his own.

• To run inside for the toy, turn to page 16.
• To stay in the shelter, turn to page 21.

Before your parents can stop you, you dash out of the shelter. You run up the back steps as fresh explosions hit the ground a few blocks away, creating bursts of heat and flames.

Inside the house, your heart beats with fear as you frantically search for Mr. Booboo. Finally, you spot the toy rabbit! You grab him and run back into the shelter.

Papa and Mama are very angry, but mostly they're relieved you aren't hurt.

"Never do such a thing again," Papa says sternly. "It is too dangerous!"

"I promise," you reply shakily. You've never been so scared in your life!

By morning, the bombs stop, and it's safe to go back to your house. After breakfast, Mama pulls out her ration book. When the war started, the British government was afraid that food would run out. They began to ration it so everyone would have enough to eat. Every person gets a ration book. The coupons inside can be traded for certain foods.

"Run to the market and fetch me milk and cheese," she says, giving you some ration coupons.

You slip them in your pocket and run out the door. At the store, the grocer greets you kindly. You hand him the coupons, and he gives you a bottle of milk and a small packet of cheese.

It's a beautiful morning, and you decide to take your time going home. You wander through town, doing your best to ignore the damaged buildings, piles of charred wood, and broken glass in the streets. As you walk, you notice a crowd of people looking at something.

- To see what the people are looking at, turn to page 18.
- To continue home, turn to page 19.

Curious, you step closer. You glimpse a large, black object lying in the street. Before you can register what it is, someone shouts, "It's a bomb!"

You remember Papa telling you that some German bombs don't explode at first. They can sit for hours—or even days—before going off. He also told you that unexploded bombs are very dangerous.

You turn just as a deafening explosion erupts. You fly through the air and land on the street, but you don't feel any pain. It's hard to move, and you feel very, very tired. Mama and Papa's faces swim in front of you. You're filled with love for them as you close your eyes and take your last breath.

THE END

To follow another path, turn to page 9.
To learn more about the Blitz of World War II, turn to page 99.

You know your mother will be waiting, so you continue on. Soon, you spy some of your schoolmates climbing through mounds of broken bricks, concrete, and metal. You run over, relieved to see them alive! But not everyone was as lucky. You learn your friend Sarah and her whole family died when a bomb hit their flat. It's strange to think you'll never see her again.

You all play tag, and it feels good to laugh and run. But after a while, you say goodbye and head toward home. On the way, you start feeling dizzy. Your stomach hurts, and the world seems to tilt in crazy angles. When you finally make it home, Mama takes your temperature.

"You have a fever," she says. She tucks you into bed and calls the doctor, who says he'll be right over.

The afternoon stretches on as you pass in and out of consciousness. Mama gets more anxious as

Turn the page.

the sun sets. But the doctor never comes. Maybe he forgot. Maybe he's helping others. No one knows.

"We've got to get her to the hospital before the Luftwaffe comes," Mama says.

"Right," Papa replies. "We should be safe there."

You're so sick that you barely know what's happening. Soon, you're all in the car, zigzagging through damaged streets. Then the dreadful whine of the bombers fills the air.

"Faster!" Mama cries.

At that moment, a bomb lands on the road. It explodes with a thunderous roar. The only blessing is that you don't feel anything as your whole family dies in an instant.

THE END

To follow another path, turn to page 9.
To learn more about the Blitz of World War II, turn to page 99.

Mr. Booboo is not worth risking your life. You decide to stay put. After a few hours, the explosions die down. George settles down. It's quieter now, so you try to get some sleep.

Suddenly, a tremendous explosion jerks you awake. George starts to scream. Shrapnel and debris rain down onto the shelter's metal roof.

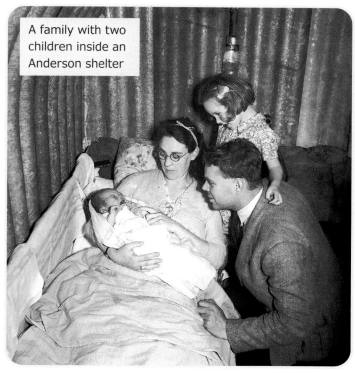

A family with two children inside an Anderson shelter

Turn the page.

After a while, the attack comes to an end. It's oddly quiet.

You feel relieved to be alive, but then Papa tries to open the shelter door. It won't open!

"We're trapped in here," he says.

"Are we buried forever?" you ask, trembling.

Mama forces a smile. "I'm sure someone will come and dig us out soon."

All night and most of the next day, you yell for help and bang on the metal walls of the shelter. But no one comes.

Eventually, Papa manages to push the door open a few inches. The opening is far too small for him to climb through. You might be able to get through, though. But by now it's almost evening again. The bombings will start soon.

• To squeeze out and run for help, go to page 23.
• To stay and wait for rescue, turn to page 25.

"I can get through," you say. "I'll go get help."

"All right." Mama hugs you tightly. "Go straight to the police station as fast as you can."

Carefully, you squeeze through the narrow opening. You're shocked at what you see outside the shelter. Many of the houses on your block—including yours—are damaged. Your shelter is buried under a pile of wreckage.

There's no time to waste. You run to the police station, arriving just as the first wave of bombers fills the sky.

"Whoa," an officer says as you burst inside. "What seems to be the problem?"

Quickly, you tell him about the shelter and your family trapped inside.

"I'll send help as soon as the attack is over," he promises.

Turn the page.

You're worried sick about your family, but you have no choice. You have to wait.

As soon as the all-clear sirens go off, a rescue team heads out. Hours later, they come back, grim-faced. Your heart stops as the officer gives you the terrible news: a bomb went off near the shelter. Your whole family is gone.

At first, you don't believe him. Your family can't be dead. They were safe in the shelter! But the sad look on his face tells you that it's real.

"Do you have any relatives?" he asks gently.

Numbly, you tell him about your Aunt Gracie in Canada. A few days later, you're on a ship bound for Canada. You're leaving London—and everything you've ever known—behind.

THE END

To follow another path, turn to page 9.
To learn more about the Blitz of World War II,
turn to page 99.

You know you can get through the opening. But you don't want to leave your family or be outside when the bombs fall either. You decide to stay put.

Soon, attacks start again. The shelter trembles with each explosion. After a time, the Luftwaffe moves to another part of the city.

Exhausted from fear and stress, you fall asleep. Then you awaken to a loud voice outside shouting, "Ho there! Anyone alive in there?"

"Yes! Yes!" Papa shouts back, pounding on the metal roof.

"Over here, boys!" the voice outside says. "We've got survivors!"

Scraping sounds come from above as the rescue team pulls the wreckage away. Soon, Papa opens the door. An ARP warden is standing there. He helps everyone out of the shelter.

Turn the page.

As your eyes adjust to the bright sunlight, you're stunned by what you see. The shelter was buried by debris from your own house.

"I'm afraid your house is ruined," the man says sadly.

"What are we going to do?" Mama asks wearily.

"You'll be evacuated out of London," the man continues. "You'll stay with another family."

As your family climbs onto a rescuer's truck, you turn to say goodbye to what's left of the only home you've ever known. You don't know what will happen next, but at least your family is alive.

THE END

To follow another path, turn to page 9.
To learn more about the Blitz of World War II, turn to page 99.

Mama decides to go to an underground Tube station. The Tube—nicknamed because of the shape of the tunnels—is a network of trains that travel beneath London's streets. Every night, hundreds of Londoners go to the stations to stay safe from the bombings.

"I want to be useful," Papa says. "When you go into the station, I'll see if the Air Raid Precaution wardens need help." ARP wardens watch for bombers, help the injured, and guide people to safety during an attack.

"I don't like it," Mama says, frowning. "I'll worry about you."

"I won't do anything rash, I promise," Papa says. "I feel better knowing you're safe."

Papa leaves for the air raid station as you help Mama gather blankets, food, and other items. When everything is ready, Mama scoops

Turn the page.

People sheltering in a London Tube station in 1940

up George, and you all make your way to the nearest Tube station. There's a long line of people waiting to get in. As you wait, you overhear some women talking nearby.

"I hear this Tube station is full!" one says. "There won't be any room for us by the time we get to the front of the line."

"Pish posh," another woman says, shaking her head. "These Tube stations are huge. There's plenty of room for everyone, and then some!"

• To stay in line, go to page 29.
• To find another shelter, turn to page 31.

Mama doesn't think the Tube station will fill up, so you all stay put. Finally, the line begins to move. Slowly and orderly, everyone makes their way down several flights of stairs to a large station platform. The air is filled with chatter as people find a spot to settle in for the night.

Once you've claimed a place on the platform, Mama tends to baby George. You find other children to play with. Women walk by with baskets full of refreshments. Far above, you hear explosions, but they're muffled and distant.

Finally, people begin settling down for the night. It's crowded and uncomfortable—and there's a lot of snoring—but at least you feel safe from the German bombs.

The next morning, Mama wakes you. You help her pack your things for the walk home. Papa meets you at the house. You jump into his arms and hug him tightly. He smells like smoke

Turn the page.

and sweat, but you don't care. He gives Mama a tired smile and tells her about the fires he helped to put out last night.

"How did the station work out?" he asks.

"I think we'll go there every night," Mama says.

Papa nods. "I'll have peace of mind knowing you'll be safe."

You're happy to hear it. Sleeping in a Tube station every night isn't much fun, but your family will manage like everyone else.

THE END

To follow another path, turn to page 9.
To learn more about the Blitz of World War II, turn to page 99.

People entering a basement bomb shelter in London

"I've heard some people are taking shelter in a bank nearby," a lady in line says.

Mama doesn't want to wait, so she leads you to the basement of the bank. It's small and full of people. The smell of sweat and dirty diapers makes your stomach heave.

"Here! Over here!" Mrs. Caldwell, your next door neighbor, waves you over. She makes room, and Mama gratefully sits beside her. Reluctantly, you sit down too.

Turn the page.

The air feels thick with fear, and everyone talks in whispers. Soon, you hear the thud of bombs landing, followed by explosions. The building shakes, and plaster rains down. You lean against Mama's shoulder and try not to be afraid.

After a while, the bombs stop.

"I need to go to the bathroom," you whisper to Mama.

She shakes her head. "We can't leave until the all-clear siren sounds," she whispers back. "There's a bucket in the corner. You'll have to use that for now."

You make your way over and find the bucket is filled to overflowing. It's disgusting. But you really need to use the bathroom.

- To use the bucket, go to page 33.
- To sneak out to find a bathroom, turn to page 35.

You hold your nose and quickly use the bucket. You throw a rag over it when you're done and then pick your way back to Mama, carefully stepping over sleeping people. After an hour or so, a siren wails—signaling the all-clear.

Relieved, you follow Mama back home. Papa comes out to greet you. He's covered with grime and soot. You give him a big hug anyway.

"That was a bad night," he says to Mama. "I spent the whole time at the docks putting out fires. But so much was destroyed, and I'm afraid it'll get worse. I think it's time we left London."

"Where are we going?" you ask, excited at the idea of leaving the war behind.

"Your Uncle James lives in the country. He offered to take us in when the bombings started," Papa replies. "He said we're welcome any time. I think we'll take him up on his offer."

Turn the page.

Moving quickly, you all pack as much as you can. Papa drives to the train station. You manage to find seats on a crowded train leaving London. As it pulls out of the station, you turn to Papa.

"How long will we be with Uncle James?" you ask.

"Until it's safe to come back," Papa replies. He looks sad. "That might be a long time."

By the time darkness falls, you're far away from London. You don't know if you'll ever see your home again, but you can't think about that now. All that matters is that your family is together and safe from the war.

THE END

To follow another path, turn to page 9.
To learn more about the Blitz of World War II, turn to page 99.

Surely the attack has stopped by now. And you really need to use the bathroom! You spot another door at the back of the basement. Before Mama can see or stop you, you step out and climb the steep stairs.

When you get outside, you stop, stunned. Almost every building is on fire. The red flames shine brightly against the dark sky. You run until you find a shop that hasn't been too damaged. You step over the glass and find the bathroom.

Explosions suddenly rock the building. Across the street, a bomb explodes—throwing flames everywhere. You know you need to get back to the shelter—coming out here was a mistake—but you're afraid to move.

- To stay where you are, turn to page 36.
- To run back to the shelter, turn to page 37.

There's a big, heavy counter in the shop, so you crouch underneath it. The sound of crackling flames gets closer. Your heart pounds with fear. You don't know what to do! Then you hear shouts. You peek over the counter and see firemen outside the building. They are yelling and spraying water on the fire.

Relief sweeps over your body. You take a chance and run to the front of the shop just as another bomb explodes nearby. A wave of intense heat and flames envelops you. The end comes so fast that you don't have time to be scared or feel any pain.

THE END

To follow another path, turn to page 9.
To learn more about the Blitz of World War II, turn to page 99.

A part of the ceiling crashes down and frightens you into action. You've got to get back to Mama! You blindly run out, dodging flames and debris. The deafening roar of the flames fills the air. All you can think about is getting away.

Finally, you stop, confused. Nothing looks familiar. Overhead, you hear the whistle of a falling bomb. A terrific explosion throws you to the ground. The world goes black.

When you wake, it's morning. You try to push yourself up, and a blinding pain shoots up your arm. Slowly, you stand and look around. Twisted, burnt cars are scattered along the street.

Then you spot a familiar face. "Papa!" you cry.

Your father rushes to you, tears streaming down his face. Mama and George are close behind. You cling to Mama, crying with joy and relief. She is crying too.

Turn the page.

"We've been looking for you all night!" Papa exclaims, pulling you into his strong arms. "It's a miracle you're alive."

"They are evacuating children from the city," Mama says. "I've decided you must go. I can't go through this worry again."

"Where will I go?" you ask nervously.

"Someplace safe and far away from the awful bombings," Mama says. "Thousands of children are being evacuated from London. You'll stay with a family who will take good care of you until it's safe to come home."

"What about George?" you ask.

"George is too little to go," Mama replies.

The next few days go by quickly. After a doctor sets your broken arm, Mama packs what you need: a change of clothes, a nightgown, a toothbrush, a comb, and your winter coat.

Then, one morning, Papa and Mama take you to the train station. Hundreds of children and their families crowd the platform. A kind lady pins a name tag onto your coat.

Tearfully, you cling to Papa and Mama. "I don't want to leave!" you sob.

Mama wipes your tears and her own. "We will visit you and write letters," she says. "I'm sure our brave army will defeat Hitler soon. Then you'll be able to come home."

The lady leads you to your seat, and the train pulls out of the station. You don't know who you'll be staying with, but you hope they're nice. And you're worried about your family. All you can do is pray they'll survive until this horrible war is over.

THE END

To follow another path, turn to page 9.
To learn more about the Blitz of World War II,
turn to page 99.

CHAPTER 3

DOING YOUR PART TO PROTECT OTHERS

Liverpool, England, is a lovely, midsize city. It is also one of Great Britain's most vital ports, and you can't imagine living anywhere else. After you graduated from school, you got a job working at a downtown dress shop. It's a good, quiet life.

Then, in 1939, everything changes. Adolf Hitler orders the German army to invade Poland. The attack marks the beginning of World War II. Two days after the invasion, Great Britain and France declare war on Germany.

Turn the page.

Now it's 1940, and Hitler has decided to attack Great Britain. For the past few weeks, the Luftwaffe—the German Air Force—has attacked Liverpool almost every night. The city is a prime Nazi target because millions of tons of food and goods from other countries come to Great Britain through Liverpool. Hitler's goal is to destroy the port so no cargo ships can enter to bring supplies or leave. Thousands of people have died. Hundreds of buildings have been destroyed. Hitler hopes this will terrorize and demoralize the British people so badly that Great Britain will surrender.

You want to help Liverpool and its people, so you volunteer as an ARP warden. Most wardens are men, but they've also accepted thousands of women like you. Wardens help protect people before and during German attacks, and you like being useful to the war effort. Each night after work at the dress shop, you grab your gas mask and put on a metal helmet and an arm band. These identify you as a warden. Then you patrol neighborhoods—watching for the Luftwaffe, handing out gas masks, giving first aid, and doing whatever jobs need doing.

You're on duty tonight, so you head to your local warden station. Every neighborhood is divided into sectors, each with its own warden station. The stations are stocked with gas masks, gas suits, electric flashlights, a first-aid kit, and other equipment.

Each night, between three and six wardens are on the job—both men and women. You greet the other wardens and then see what jobs need to be done. You could patrol the area. Or, you could volunteer for watch duty.

• To go on patrol, turn to page 44.
• To go on watch duty, turn to page 58.

Your main job on patrol is making sure all the lights in your sector are turned out. Luftwaffe pilots use lights on the ground to locate targets. So, each night, the city turns off the streetlights. Every building goes dark. Even automobile headlights are covered. People also hang blackout curtains in their windows and stay indoors.

Hurriedly, you walk through your sector's neighborhoods, checking for even the tiniest speck of light. If you see any, you knock on the door, shouting, "Turn out the lights, and get those curtains up!"

By the time you've made your rounds, it's fully dark. Suddenly, warning sirens wail throughout the city. The low drone of German airplane engines gets louder. Fear jumps up your throat, but you swallow it. No time to be afraid now.

Everyone in town is assigned to an air raid shelter, and you run to the one you're in charge of. You pull out a list of names and check people off as they arrive. There's one person missing! It's Frank, an elderly man you know well.

A woman runs out of the shelter and grabs your sleeve.

"My daughter Betty isn't here," she says frantically. She gives you Betty's full name, and you check your list.

"Betty's name is checked off right here," you say reassuringly.

"Yes, she signed in with me," Betty's mother replies. "But she's gone now! She must have gone back to the house."

You need to get these last two people into the shelter before the bombs fall.

- To go to Frank's house, turn to page 46.
- To find Betty, turn to page 48.

Quickly, you dash to Frank's tiny house and knock loudly on his door. He opens it a crack and peeks through.

"Go away!" he shouts. "Leave me alone!"

"Frank," you say, "you're not safe in there by yourself. Please come with me."

"No!" he responds. "I hate those shelters. Too crowded and too smelly!"

A female ARP warden walks through the rubble left by an air raid in 1940.

You nod. "I don't like them much, either," you admit.

The rumble of plane engines is closer. You hear the dreaded whistle of bombs dropping. One hits a few blocks away, and a fiery explosion lights the sky.

"Please, Frank," you say, reaching out your hand. "Let's go now."

"All right," he finally agrees.

You push the door open and take Frank's arm. As you step onto the sidewalk, an incendiary bomb lands in the street, spewing flames. The last thing you feel is Frank's hand gripping your arm as the fire engulfs you both. At least you aren't alone at the end.

THE END

To follow another path, turn to page 9.
To learn more about the Blitz of World War II, turn to page 99.

"Don't worry," you tell the woman calmly. "I'll fetch your daughter. It's safer for you here."

Thankfully, Betty's house isn't far away. When you get there, you find a teenage girl and a small dog huddled in the backyard.

"You must be Betty," you say. "Come with me. Your mum's waiting for you at the shelter."

"I won't leave Buster behind!" Betty cries.

Dogs aren't usually allowed in bomb shelters. But you must get Betty to safety.

"All right," you say. "Bring him along."

Betty jumps up, clutching the small dog in her arms. When you get to the shelter, you turn to the frightened girl.

"Tuck him into your coat," you say, giving the dog a pat on the head. "Keep him quiet and hidden until it's over."

"Thank you!" she says. Then she ducks into the shelter.

Just then, Mildred, another warden, spies you. "We've got reports of people trapped in their Anderson shelter," she says, pressing a scrap of paper into your hand. "This is the address."

Anderson shelters are small metal bomb shelters buried halfway underground. They hold three or four people, so many families have them.

You get to the address and look for the Anderson shelter, but there's nothing here! Before you can move, an incendiary bomb explodes a few blocks away. A few minutes later, a fire truck zooms toward the fire, bells clanging.

You have no idea where the trapped family might be. It's unlikely you'll ever find them now. But you might be of some use to the firemen.

• To keep looking for the family, turn to page 50.
• To help the firefighters, turn to page 56.

Finding the family is your first priority. You spot a row of damaged homes a block or two away. Each house has a tiny garden, or backyard. Most people build their Anderson shelters in their gardens. Maybe the family you're looking for is there.

When you arrive, you dash back and forth between the small houses, looking for an Anderson shelter. Panic churns your stomach as the Luftwaffe's planes roar overhead and then disappear. When you get to the last house in the row, you hear muffled banging and voices coming from the garden. "Help! Help!"

You scour the yard and finally spot the shelter. The door is blocked by a large tree branch. You pull on it with all your strength. Finally, the branch moves just enough to get the shelter door open. A man, woman, and two little girls emerge from inside.

You're relieved to see that no one is injured, but the feeling is short-lived. The squad of German planes returns, screeching by overhead. Bombs could fall any minute.

"Follow me," you say, glancing worriedly at the dark sky. "We don't have much time."

"Wait!" the woman cries. "There may be others next door."

It's your job to search for survivors who need help. But it's also your duty to get this family to safety.

- To search for more survivors, turn to page 52.
- To take this family to the shelter, turn to page 55.

If there are more survivors, you must find them.

"I'll look," you say. "Get to the air raid shelter as fast as you can."

The man nods, and he and his family run.

You scramble over splintered lumber and piles of bricks, shouting, "Hello! Anyone here?" But no one answers.

The Luftwaffe's planes drop low and release more bombs. One lands across the street. A terrific explosion sends you flying backward. You land hard, and everything goes dark.

When you open your eyes, it's daylight. Painfully, you get to your feet. The whole block has been destroyed. There's nothing left but piles of rubble. You can't believe you're alive.

Police help dazed residents through the debris. Crews are working to clear the streets. One man

People walking next to ruined houses after a bombing raid in Liverpool

drops his shovel and shouts. He's found a body. It's the woman you rescued from the Anderson shelter. You sink to the ground in shock and cover your eyes. You know they're going to find the rest of that poor family, and you can't bear to watch. The full impact of what you're seeing hits you so hard you can't breathe. If you'd been with them, you'd be dead too.

Turn the page.

Gently, the workers load the bodies into a truck. The crew will take the bodies somewhere to be identified. Hopefully, friends or family will claim them to be buried. Sadly, many bodies aren't identified. They will be buried in a mass grave with others killed in the bombings.

It's too much. That afternoon, you pack a bag and board a train to the country. You'll stay with a friend until the bombings are over. As you leave Liverpool, you hope you never see the terrible effects of this war again.

THE END

To follow another path, turn to page 9.
To learn more about the Blitz of World War II,
turn to page 99.

You decide to get this family to safety. But you need to move fast.

"This way!" you shout, dashing toward a nearby shop. You'll be much safer indoors. The five of you hurry inside and huddle in a corner as the bombers dive lower.

Boom! A bomb explodes in the street. The shop walls shake, sending a cloud of plaster into the air.

Boom! The next bomb lands in front of the shop. The ceiling collapses with a crash, trapping you all in the corner. Too late, you realize that coming in here was a terrible mistake.

The next bomb lands on the shop roof and falls through the damaged ceiling. You don't have time to be afraid as the explosion rips the shop apart.

THE END

To follow another path, turn to page 9.
To learn more about the Blitz of World War II,
turn to page 99.

By the time you get to the burning building, fire trucks are already there. Long water hoses snake across the road. Firemen shoot streams of water at the flames. Sparks from the fire fall like burning rain, starting several smaller fires.

"Come on!" a fireman shouts, grabbing a stirrup pump.

Stirrup pumps are large metal buckets filled with water that have a hose and pump attached.

Firefighters putting out blazes during the Blitz

They're used for battling small fires. It's important to put out these little fires so they don't spread.

The fireman pumps the water while you point the hose. When that fire is out, you quickly put out another, then another.

By dawn, the attack is over—and all the fires are out. But as the sun rises, you see the destruction clearly. A few buildings still stand, but most have been reduced to rubble. Weary residents stare in shock at the remains of their burned-out homes.

Exhaustion and sadness overwhelm you as you make your way back to the warden station to write your report. But no matter how hard it is, you'll be back tomorrow night. It's your duty to save lives, and that's what you'll do—for as long as you can.

THE END

To follow another path, turn to page 9.
To learn more about the Blitz of World War II, turn to page 99.

You make your way to the roof of a nearby building for watch duty and join a spotter who is already there. Spotters scan the skies, looking for incoming Nazi bombing squads.

As the sun begins to set, tiny black specks appear in the distant sky. Your heart jumps.

"Are those bombers?" you cry, pointing.

"They sure are," the spotter replies as he consults his maps. "They'll be in the city in about ten minutes. But based on their position, I think they'll turn south tonight."

Sirens begin to blare throughout the city.

"I have to stay here and monitor their position," he says. "I could use help."

You should be at the warden station during an air raid. Then again, maybe you should stay to help.

- To go back to the warden station, go to page 59.
- To help the spotter, turn to page 66.

"I'm really sorry, but I'm needed at the warden station," you say.

The spotter nods. "I can handle it, don't worry," he says.

You dash through the streets to your station. By the time you arrive, the other wardens are helping people into the air raid shelters and checking names off their lists.

Gerald, the senior warden, takes your report that the bombers are flying south.

"We need to make sure everyone has been evacuated," he says. "Take my bicycle, and check your assigned sector," he says. "Then check these streets too."

He hands you a scrap of paper covered with a hastily-scribbled list.

"These streets aren't in my sector," you say, puzzled.

Turn the page.

Three young men at an ARP warden station

"Another station lost a warden last night," Gerald says sadly. "We've been asked to cover her sector until they get a replacement warden."

This is terrible news, but you don't have time for grief. You jump on the bike, and off you go. Most houses are empty. The families you do find sheltering in their homes have their blackout curtains drawn. You also find a few families inside Anderson shelters. The same goes for the areas in the other warden's sector. When you're finished, you turn back toward your station.

The other warden's sector is in an unfamiliar area of town, but you're not too worried since the Luftwaffe's planes flew south. You make a couple of wrong turns when bombers suddenly fill the air. The Luftwaffe's planes are here after all!

Moments later, a bomb crashes onto the road. Miraculously, it doesn't explode. But you can't go that way now.

Trying to stay calm, you turn in the opposite direction, biking away from the unexploded bomb as quickly as you can. You zoom around a corner and see a sign that says, "Warden Station." Beside it is a wall of sandbags protecting a small shop. You could stay there until the attack is over. Or, you could take your chances and head back to your own station.

• To go to the closer station, turn to page 62.
• To keep biking to your own station, turn to page 64.

The sooner you can get to safety, the better, so you opt for the closer station. You throw the bike down and run through the door just as another bomb detonates. Inside, two wardens and many civilians are crowded into the narrow space. Without a word, they make room for you.

British civilians in a packed air raid shelter in 1940

The bombing seems to go on forever, but at least you're safe. Finally, at dawn, the explosions stop. The all-clear sirens go off. Slowly, everyone steps out to see the damage. Several small fires burn here and there, but most of the area escaped destruction.

You're relieved. It could have been a lot worse. Wearily, you climb onto the bike. It's still dim, but you're sure you can find your way back to the station.

You're halfway down the block when something large and dark suddenly looms in front of you in the middle of the road. Your heart stops.

"An unexploded bomb!" you shout. Frantically, you jerk the handlebars around, but you're going too fast to avoid crashing into the bomb. It explodes, and you become another casualty of this terrible war.

THE END

To follow another path, turn to page 9.
To learn more about the Blitz of World War II,
turn to page 99.

You pedal as hard as you can and turn the next corner. Relief washes over you—you recognize this block! It's not far to your own station, but it's too dangerous to ride in the street. You'd be unprotected out in the open. Instead, you hop the curb and ride down the sidewalk.

In the flickering light of the fires, you see something floating in the air. It's a parachute mine—the deadliest of all German bombs.

You have to get as far away as you can. You begin pedaling furiously and don't even hear the explosion when it comes. Suddenly, you feel weightless, flying through the air.

The next thing you know, you're sitting in the middle of the street. Lying nearby is a tangle of twisted metal and rubber. It's all that's left of the bike.

It's a miracle you weren't killed in that blast. Dazed, you get up and start walking.

Gerald's eyes widen in shock when he sees you finally arrive back at the station. "You're covered in blood!" he cries.

"I'm okay," you say, but it's hard to talk. "There was a parachute mine . . ."

That's the last thing you remember as you collapse. You wake up in a hospital, covered in bandages. Your time as an air raid warden is over, but at least you're still alive.

THE END

To follow another path, turn to page 9.
To learn more about the Blitz of World War II,
turn to page 99.

"I can stay," you say crisply. "I'm sure the other wardens have things under control at the station."

The spotter nods and bends over a pile of maps. You take over the telephone and relay information to other spotters. They call back with reports and updates.

You're looking at the maps when the telephone jangles again. A frantic voice on the other end shouts, "The bombers have turned around! They're headed your way!"

"The Luftwaffe is coming!" you shout, slamming down the receiver. "What do I do?"

"Call it in!" the spotter says quickly. "Then get back to your station."

You make the call, and a few minutes later sirens go off, warning of the coming attack.

You head to the ladder and look behind you. The spotter hasn't moved.

"Aren't you coming with me?" you ask. "It's not safe up here on the roof. You need to get somewhere safe."

"I need to stay here and monitor the squad," he replies. "Thanks for your help. I'll be fine."

By the time you get back to the station, the attack has started—and it's chaos. Fire trucks tear through the streets as people push to get inside a shelter. The bombs sound far away, but you know they're getting closer.

An ambulance pulls up, and a warden you don't know stumbles out. He's covered in blood. You rush over to help him.

"Driver . . . killed . . . ," he croaks. "I must . . . go . . ."

Turn the page.

"You're not going anywhere except to a hospital," you say.

He desperately grabs your sleeve.

"Shelter in the school basement . . . lots of people . . . hit hard," he says. "Whole block . . . businesses on fire . . . people trapped everywhere."

He mumbles a street name and then collapses.

"Help! I need help here!" you shout. Gerald, the senior warden, rushes to help you. Quickly, you explain what the man said.

"I know the place," you say, grabbing the ambulance keys.

"Go," Gerald replies. "I can take care of him." A quick look inside the ambulance tells you that it's fully stocked and ready. But where should you go first?

• To go to the school, go to page 69.
• To go to the business buildings, turn to page 72.

When you arrive at the school, a frightening scene greets you. More than half the school has been destroyed. Fires burn in the wreckage, their heat stinging your skin. Some firefighters battle the flames while police officers dig through the rubble to find survivors. The Luftwaffe's planes are gone, though. Hopefully, no more bombs will fall here tonight.

Rescue workers climbing over the ruins of a school in Liverpool after a German air raid in 1941

Turn the page.

You run up to one officer. "How many people were in there?" you ask breathlessly.

"Not sure," he replies tiredly. "Couple hundred, maybe? The bomb went all the way down to the basement and burst gas lines and heating boilers."

So many injured! There's already a group of injured people gathered on the street. Quickly, you begin assessing the injuries. Minor wounds can be cared for here. People who are more seriously injured will be taken to the hospital.

You lose track of time as you focus on helping as many people as possible. You barely notice when another ambulance appears to take people to the hospital. By sunrise, you're out of supplies.

"I need to get more bandages and other things," you tell the other ambulance driver.

He puts his hand on your arm and shakes his head. "No need. There aren't any more injured."

"But I saw firemen bring people out on stretchers," you reply, confused.

The young man looks at you sadly. "Those folks don't need help anymore."

Instantly, you understand. Those people are no longer alive. They died in a shelter, where they thought they'd be safe.

The young man gives you a tired smile. "We saved a lot of people tonight. That's something."

We did save people, you think as you pack up. But it never feels like enough. So tomorrow, you'll come back and try again.

THE END

To follow another path, turn to page 9.
To learn more about the Blitz of World War II,
turn to page 99.

By the time you get there, the entire block of businesses is engulfed in flames. It's hard to breathe from the smoke in the air. Firemen rush here and there, pointing hoses at the fire. Several injured people are sitting or lying in the street. One by one, you clean their wounds. A fireman helps load these people into your ambulance.

For the rest of the night, you drive to and from the hospital. Another ambulance shows up, and you and the other driver take turns helping the injured and taking others to the hospital. Together, you save dozens of people.

Finally, the fires are out. The other ambulance driver takes the last of the injured away. The firemen begin packing their equipment. You pack up the ambulance and get ready to go back to the station. You have a report to write.

A cool breeze fans your face, and you breathe in fresh air. But then you smell something else.

"Is that gas?" you call over to the firemen.

Gas is highly flammable. A gas leak near a fire is very dangerous.

A fireman heads toward you and then stops. A look of horror crosses his face as he smells it too.

Without warning, an enormous explosion rips through the block. You're thrown backward. Your head hits a wall. Your last thought is of the people you helped save that night. You made a difference, and that counts for something.

THE END

To follow another path, turn to page 9.
To learn more about the Blitz of World War II, turn to page 99.

CHAPTER 4

A WALL OF FIRE AND DEATH

You grew up in Coventry, a very old city in central England. In the Middle Ages, it had castles and cathedrals. Now, Coventry is filled with factories that make everything from bicycles to automobiles.

When World War II started about a year ago, many factories switched to making war supplies like ammunition and airplane parts. Because of this, Coventry is now one of the most important industrial cities in England. Unfortunately, it also makes the city a prime target for Adolf Hitler. The Nazis want to destroy Coventry's factories to keep these supplies from the British army.

Turn the page.

You wanted to join the army and fight the Germans, but you were rejected because of an old injury. Instead, you volunteered for the Auxiliary Fire Service. For the past year, you've battled bombing fires from Luftwaffe attacks almost every night. It's dangerous and dirty work. But you're glad you can be of service to your beloved city and your country.

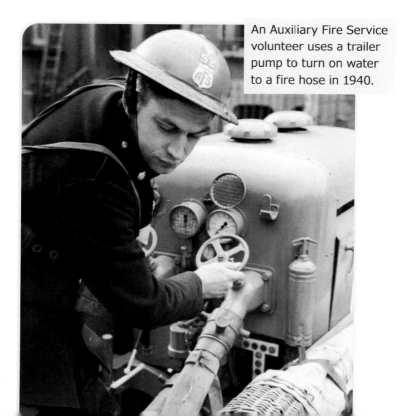

An Auxiliary Fire Service volunteer uses a trailer pump to turn on water to a fire hose in 1940.

On November 14, 1940, you report for duty before sunset. The Luftwaffe's attacks usually come after dark. The city's warning sirens go off around 7:00 at night. Almost instantly, the bombing starts.

The sky is filled with more planes than you've ever seen. Panic rises in your throat as incendiary bombs rain down. Tonight, the Germans are not just targeting the factories—they seem to be attacking the whole city!

Fires are breaking out everywhere. Frantic calls come into the station about factories in flames. One of the city's oldest and most beautiful cathedrals, St. Michael's Cathedral, is also getting bombarded.

You could join the crew fighting the factory fires. Or, you could go with a crew to save the cathedral.

• To go to the factory, turn to page 78.
• To go to the cathedral, turn to page 87.

You're on a five-man Auxiliary team. Each team has a fire pump. This heavy piece of equipment on wheels must be pulled to a fire by another vehicle. Once the pump is at the fire, it's attached to a fire hydrant.

Unfortunately, you don't have a fire truck to get the pump to the fire. Instead, you call a taxi! Taxis are large, sturdy vehicles. They're strong enough to pull the heavy pumps. When the taxi arrives, you and the other firemen quickly hook the pump onto the cab. The cab driver takes you and your team straight to the fire.

When you get to the factory, you and the other firemen attach the hoses and aim the water into the blaze. The bottom floors seem undamaged. There might be survivors there. But the top half of the factory is engulfed in flames.

- To check for survivors, go to page 79.
- To keep fighting the fire, turn to page 81.

It's a long shot, but you have to check and see if anyone is alive. Inside, the factory floor is filled with huge machinery. It's hard to see through the smoke.

"Anyone here?" you shout.

"Here! Here!" comes a faint reply.

There's a locked door at the back. You break it open. Some factory workers huddle in a corner.

"Thank the lord!" one says. "We thought we'd be safe from the bombs here!"

You lead them out quickly, coughing from the smoke.

"More . . . inside . . . ," a woman gasps, trying to breathe.

You make sure these survivors are safe and then run back inside. By now, the fire has spread. Flames lick at the walls. A deafening *crack* comes

Turn the page.

from somewhere above you. You glance up just as a large roof beam falls, pinning you to the floor. Flames race through the room so fast you don't have time to be afraid—or feel pain as you perish in the fire.

THE END

To follow another path, turn to page 9.
To learn more about the Blitz of World War II,
turn to page 99.

Suddenly, an explosion erupts inside the factory. The roof collapses, and the fire quickly spreads. No one could survive that.

You keep fighting the fire. But no matter how hard you try, the flames grow bigger. The Luftwaffe's planes thunder overhead, dropping more bombs. It seems like the whole city is on fire!

Then, without warning, the water stops flowing. The hose goes limp.

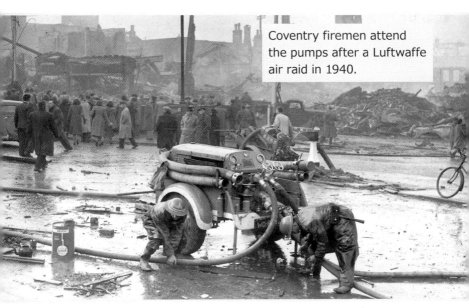

Coventry firemen attend the pumps after a Luftwaffe air raid in 1940.

Turn the page.

"No water!" the other firemen shout. "All the water's gone!"

You can't believe it, but they're right. All the hoses deflate. Only a trickle of water comes out.

You have no idea what happened. But no water means there's no way to fight any more fires. You stare at the wall of flames, helpless to do anything. Numbly, you start rolling up the hoses so they don't get burned.

"Hey, can I have some help over here?" the chief shouts.

You hurry over and see one of the other firemen on the ground. He's badly burned.

"Someone needs to get him to a hospital," the chief says. "I could take him. But someone must lead the others in case the water comes back on."

• To volunteer to go to the hospital, go to page 83.
• To volunteer to take command, turn to page 85.

The hospital is in a state of chaos when you arrive. Doctors and nurses frantically race from one injured person to another. People are shouting for help and crying in pain. Others sit, dazed and wrapped in bandages.

You stop a doctor, who gives the injured firefighter a quick exam.

"He's got burns on his hands, feet, and neck," the doctor finally says. "One of the nurses will take care of him. You should go. There's nothing you can do for him."

"It looks like you could use help here," you reply. "I have first-aid training."

The doctor smiles at you gratefully. "There are injured people waiting in the front."

For the next several hours, you tend to the injured. Some only need a few bandages. Others have serious burns or shrapnel wounds. When

Turn the page.

you finally run out of supplies, it's dawn. The worst attack you've ever seen is over.

Exhausted, you step outside. There is destruction everywhere. Whole blocks are gone. Smoke from the fires hangs in the air. People stumble through the devastation, looking for anything that might be left of their lives.

This terrible scene makes you even more determined to survive and defend your city. One day, Coventry will be as beautiful as it once was.

THE END

To follow another path, turn to page 9.
To learn more about the Blitz of World War II, turn to page 99.

The captain leaves for the hospital. You're supposed to organize and decide what to do next. Fires still blaze all around you. There are hundreds of other fires all over town and no water to put them out.

The most destructive German air raid on Coventry left the city in smoking ruins.

Turn the page.

You have to do something! You order some men to fan out and look for sandbags. Pouring sand on a fire can put it out. You command other men to keep the hoses attached to the hydrants, just in case the water comes back. But it's no use. There are no sandbags anywhere, and the water is gone for good.

A wave of sadness and despair washes through you. So much death all around. More people will die tomorrow when the bombers come again. It all seems so hopeless.

You turn around and begin walking. It doesn't matter where you go, as long as you're away from all the death and destruction. You disappear into the smoke and darkness to escape this horror.

THE END

To follow another path, turn to page 9.
To learn more about the Blitz of World War II, turn to page 99.

St. Michael's Cathedral is a magnificent medieval building. Its tall spires stretch to the sky. The cathedral is famous all over England—and now it's on fire.

Several Auxiliary fire crews rush to save the great cathedral, including yours. Each crew includes five firemen and a portable fire pump that can be hooked up to the fire hydrants around the city. Auxiliary fire crews don't have trucks to get to the fire. All the fire trucks are used by the professional firemen. Instead, they use taxis. British taxis are sturdy and can pull the heavy pumps. And since taxi drivers have the whole city memorized, they can get crews to fires quickly.

The taxi gets your crew to the cathedral safely. You unroll the fire hoses and get to work. The fire is big, and you work hard to get the flames under control. A few hours later, the fire is almost out. All that's left are a few smaller fires here and there,

Turn the page.

Firemen with a pump hitched to a taxi next to a burning building bombed by the Luftwaffe

but they'll be easy to put out. It looks like you've saved the cathedral! It's a relief to know that something this beautiful will escape destruction.

Just then, a bicycle messenger appears and hands you a piece of paper. The message is from the main fire station. The electricity is out, and they need help. Do you stay here and finish putting out the cathedral fire? Or, should you head back to the station?

- To stay at the cathedral, go to page 89.
- To go to the station, turn to page 96.

You send another fireman to the station and return to the last small fires at the cathedral. It doesn't take long to put them out too. You're unhooking the hoses when you hear the hated roar of the Luftwaffe's planes overhead. They're back! Before you can move, a fresh round of incendiary bombs falls out of the sky. The cathedral erupts into a ball of flames once again!

With a shout, you quickly hook the hose back up, turn on the pump, and point the water at the flames. This fire is worse than it was before, but you grit your teeth and do your job.

Desperately, the firemen try to get the blaze under control. But suddenly, the water disappears! The hoses hang limp and empty. At first, you think something is wrong with the pumps. Then another bike messenger appears.

"Bombs have destroyed gas and water services in the city," he tells you breathlessly.

Turn the page.

"What are you saying?" you shout, panic rising. "How is that possible? All the water pipes are underground."

The boy looks miserable. "A bomb exploded right above the main lines," he says. "Broke the water pipes and tore the electrical lines apart. There's no more water to fight the fires."

You refuse to accept that the water is gone. You could try and find water. But where? At that moment, a man appears with a small group of survivors. He looks familiar, but he's covered in so much soot and grime that you don't recognize him.

"Can you help us please?" the man pleads. Everyone is injured, and one woman is limping badly.

- To stay and help the survivors, go to page 91.
- To try to find more water, turn to page 94.

Your priority is to help survivors. You call another fireman over, and together you help the people into a nearby truck.

"We'll get you to a hospital," you assure the sooty man.

"Thank you," he says. His voice sounds familiar. Then you realize this man is Reverend Howard. He is the reverend of St. Michael's.

"We were inside the church when the second round of bombs hit."

You're shocked that he and the others are alive!

"What happened?" you ask.

Reverend Howard sighs. "I knew one day Coventry would be attacked," he begins. "So a few weeks ago, I put together a group of fire-watchers, the Cathedral Guard. But we weren't ready for such a big fire."

Turn the page.

"The bombs hit many parts of the cathedral," he continues. "First, we went to the roof to save the building. Then, we threw buckets of sand on the fires inside. Then more bombs fell, and we knew it was no use."

You shake your head at their foolish bravery. "You all could have died in there," you say. "But I admire your dedication to the church."

"At least we're all alive," he continues.

You see to it that Reverend Howard and the other survivors get to the hospital. By dawn, the attack is over. The all-clear siren echoes through what's left of the city. The destruction is overwhelming. All that remains of the cathedral is the tall spire and some outer walls.

The next day, King George, England's monarch, comes to Coventry to look at the damage. His sadness and anger at what the

King George (left, in uniform) visiting Coventry to survey bombing damage on November 17, 1940

Nazis have done matches your own. You're impressed that the king cared enough about Coventry to come in person. Seeing the king gives you the determination to keep fighting and the hope that England will survive this war.

THE END

To follow another path, turn to page 9.
To learn more about the Blitz of World War II, turn to page 99.

You quickly check all the nearby hydrants. There's no water anywhere. But the city has many pools, fountains, and ponds. Surely you can use the water from those!

You lead a group of firefighters to a nearby park with a large pool. The pumps work perfectly. For the rest of the night, you fight the fires with the pond water. But the fires are too big, and there are too many of them. All you can hope to do is keep them from spreading.

By dawn, the pond is almost drained. The cathedral is all but gone. All that's left is its tall, beautiful spire and a few outer walls.

You wander through the smoking ruins, exhausted and heartbroken. Then you spot two wooden beams—burnt and black—in the shape of a cross. Somehow, the sight gives you hope.

Ruins of St. Michael's Cathedral in Coventry

The people of Coventry—and of England—will keep fighting. You know in your heart you'll never give in.

THE END

To follow another path, turn to page 9.
To learn more about the Blitz of World War II,
turn to page 99.

The station is in a state of total confusion when you arrive. The electricity is out, so everyone is working by candlelight. The telephones are also dead. The only way to communicate is with the bicycle messengers. They rush in and out, dropping messages and grabbing new ones. The ground rumbles with the sound of bombers and anti-aircraft fire.

For the rest of the night, you organize the messengers and help get equipment in the right place. Just before dawn, a soot-covered messenger finds you.

"The cathedral is gone," she says sadly.

That can't be possible. "We put out that fire," you reply.

The girl shakes her head. "Maybe so, sir, but it caught fire again. Ain't nothing left but the steeple and some walls."

You have to see for yourself. When you step outside the station, you stop in shock. Huge parts of the city are gone. Some places are scraped clean to the bare earth. Other areas are filled with enormous piles of concrete, brick, wood, and metal. There are bomb craters on every street.

The cathedral spire a few blocks away rises above the ruins. As you walk toward it, your heart sinks. Most of the church is gone. A few broken walls stand above the rubble. The air smells of smoke and burnt wood.

Deep sadness wells inside your chest. Maybe there is no hope. Then anger boils over. No one can destroy your city and get away with it! You vow to do everything you can to make Hitler and the Nazis pay for what they've done.

THE END

To follow another path, turn to page 9.
To learn more about the Blitz of World War II, turn to page 99.

CHAPTER 5

THE LEGACY OF THE BLITZ

For eight terrifying months during World War II—from September 1940 to May 1941—the British people faced nightly bombings and possible death. Many ordinary people showed astounding bravery during the Blitz. Their actions helped keep up the morale of the country and showed the Nazis the strength of the British people.

The Luftwaffe hit London—England's capital city—the hardest. Nearly 30,000 Londoners were killed. Millions of homes and apartments were damaged or destroyed. Heavy bombing pounded London on the night of September 12, 1940. An unexploded bomb fell on St. Paul's Cathedral and became buried underneath it. Robert Davies, a bomb engineer, took a team to the cathedral. Their job was to disarm the bomb before it destroyed this famous landmark. But the bomb was buried too deeply to disarm safely. Davies's only choice was to remove it.

St. Paul's Cathedral defiantly towers behind buildings damaged by German bombs in December 1940.

For three long days, he and his team carefully dug out the bomb. There were damaged electrical cables and gas leaks everywhere. One wrong move and the bomb would go off. They finally got it out and loaded it onto a truck. Davies drove the bomb far away from the cathedral. Then he detonated it safely, saving the cathedral and everyone living nearby.

Liverpool was the second-hardest hit city. More than 4,000 people were killed, and 70,000 people in the city and surrounding areas were left homeless. James Henry Wheeler was an ARP warden in Liverpool during a night of heavy bombing. While he was on duty, a bomb flattened several houses. A woman and small boy were trapped. Wheeler jumped into action, propping up the debris so he could dig them out. There was a dangerous gas leak, and the house next door was on fire. Smoke filled the air, but

Wheeler put a handkerchief over his mouth and kept digging. He finally got them out and to safety.

But the worst night of the Blitz happened in Coventry on November 14, 1940. More than 500 planes attacked the city for 11 hours. The bombing was so fierce that German pilots— thousands of feet in the air—could feel the heat from the fires. After the Coventry attack, the Germans invented a new word, *coventrieren*, meaning, "to raze a city to the ground."

Brandon Moss served as a constable in Coventry. He was on duty on November 14— the night of the Luftwaffe's worst attack. That evening, a bomb hit a house and destroyed it. Moss knew there were people trapped inside. There was also a gas leak and falling debris everywhere. The situation was so dangerous that other rescuers refused to stay, but Moss wouldn't give up. He worked alone all night with bombs falling all around until he finally freed the three people trapped inside.

The Blitz was more than a plan of attack to Hitler and the Nazis. They wanted to break the morale of the British people. Hitler hoped Churchill and the British government would suffer so much they would surrender. Instead of

British Prime Minister Winston Churchill (front, with cane) surveying air raid damage in south London in September 1940

cowering in despair, the British people rose up. They defended their cities. They helped victims find food and shelter. Businesses stayed open. Children went to school. People went to movies and restaurants. It was their way of showing the Nazis that nothing would break their spirits.

The Blitz lasted until May 11, 1941. Then suddenly, Hitler called off the Blitz attacks. He ordered the Luftwaffe to go to other targets.

The British people showed remarkable resilience and determination during the Blitz.

Although the Blitz was over, this was only the beginning of World War II. A few months later, on December 7, 1941, the Japanese attacked Pearl Harbor. The next day, the United States and Great Britain declared war on Japan. Then, on December 11, Hitler declared war on the United States. World War II raged until 1945, when Germany and Japan were finally defeated.

The legacy of the Blitz is that it failed. Before the Blitz began, the world had watched in horror as Hitler and the Nazis conquered country after country in Europe. They seemed unstoppable. The Blitz pounded Great Britain so badly that everyone expected the British to surrender. But the British people survived. Hitler's failure to conquer England proved that the Nazis were not invincible. The bravery of the British people during the Blitz—and their refusal to be destroyed—was a glimmer of hope for the rest of the world that Hitler could be defeated.

Timeline of the World War II Blitz

September 1, 1939: Germany invades Poland, beginning World War II.

September 3, 1939: Great Britain and France declare war on Germany.

May 10–June 22, 1940: The Nazis use quick attacks, called *Blitzkrieg*, to conquer the Netherlands, Belgium, and northern France.

May 30, 1940: Winston Churchill becomes the prime minister of Great Britain.

September 7, 1940: A squad of Luftwaffe planes attacks London, beginning the Blitz.

September 27, 1940: Germany, Italy, and Japan join forces to create the Axis powers.

November 14, 1940: The Luftwaffe bombs Coventry, England, in the worst Blitz attack of World War II.

November 23, 1940: The city of Southampton, England, suffers a serious Blitz attack.

November 24, 1940: The Luftwaffe attacks the English city of Bristol.

November 28, 1940: Liverpool, England, suffers its first major Blitz attack.

December 12, 1940: Sheffield, England—home to many steel factories—is bombed by the Luftwaffe.

December 22–24, 1940: The Luftwaffe bombs the city of Manchester, England.

January 2, 1941: Cardiff, Wales, is bombed in a Blitz attack.

January 10, 1941: The coastal city of Portsmouth, England, is attacked.

May 11, 1941: Hitler calls off the attacks to prepare for an attack on the Soviet Union, ending the Blitz.

Other Paths to Explore

1. You are a small child during the Blitz when the British government launches Operation Pied Piper. This program hopes to protect children and keep them safe. Parents are encouraged to send their children to the countryside—far from the bombings—but they can't go with them. The children live with strangers. Moving somewhere safer sounds wonderful. But you would be far away from your family for months—maybe even years. Is being away and safe better than being in danger with the people you love?

2. You work the night shift at a bicycle factory in a big industrial English town. It's a good job, and you like where you live. Then one day, your boss tells you that the factory will be making ammunition for the war against Germany. Suddenly, your job is vital to the war effort. You're proud to do your part to help your country. But this will make your factory a prime target for the Luftwaffe's Blitz attacks. Would you keep working, hoping the bombs never come? Or is it best to quit now and save yourself?

3. You are the caretaker of a magnificent medieval cathedral. It is a famous historical landmark, and its ancient paintings and priceless artifacts mean a great deal to your city. This church has survived for centuries. But when the Luftwaffe start their terrible Blitz attacks, you're sure the cathedral will be a target. If the bombs come, you'll try to save everything you can. But staying here puts you in grave danger. Is protecting beautiful art worth dying for?

Bibliography

Britannica: The Blitz
britannica.com/event/the-Blitz

Eyewitness to History: The London Blitz, 1940
eyewitnesstohistory.com/blitz.htm

Historic England: London: The Blitz, September 1940–June 1941
historicengland.org.uk/whats-new/features/blitz-stories/london-the-blitz-september-1940-june-1941

Historic UK: The Blitz
historic-uk.com/HistoryUK/HistoryofBritain/The-Blitz

Imperial War Museum: The Blitz
iwm.org.uk/search/global?query=The+Blitz

Royal Airforce Museum: The Blitz
rafmuseum.org.uk/research/online-exhibitions/history-of-the-battle-of-britain/the-blitz

Glossary

ammunition (am-yuh-NISH-uhn)—objects fired, dropped, or detonated from a weapon

auxiliary (awg-ZIL-yuh-ree)—helping, or giving extra support

blitz (BLITS)—a swift, intense attack or bombing

constable (KON-stuh-buhl)—a British police officer

evacuate (ih-VAK-yoo-ayt)—to leave a place

incendiary (in-SEN-dee-er-ee)—used to set property on fire

Luftwaffe (LOOFT-vaa-fuh)—the German Air Force

morale (muh-RAL)—cheerful confidence in the face of hardship

precaution (pri-KAW-shuhn)—an action to prevent something bad from happening

ration (RA-shen)—a food allowance

raze (RAZE)—to demolish or destroy

sector (SEK-ter)—a part of a military area

shrapnel (SHRAP-nuhl)—bomb or shell fragments

Read More

Faust, Daniel. *World War II*. Minneapolis: Bearport Publishing Company, 2024.

Hearn, Hattie. *Tales of World War II: Amazing True Stories from the War that Shook the World*. New York: Neon Squid, 2023.

MacCarald, Clara. *Weapons of World War II*. Lake Elmo, MN: Focus Readers, 2023.

Internet Sites

Historic UK: The Blitz
historic-uk.com/HistoryUK/HistoryofBritain/The-Blitz

Imperial War Museum: The Blitz
iwm.org.uk/search/global?query=The+Blitz

Kids Discover: World War II
online.kidsdiscover.com/unit/world-war-ii

JOIN OTHER HISTORICAL ADVENTURES WITH MORE
YOU CHOOSE SEEKING HISTORY!

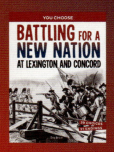

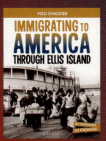

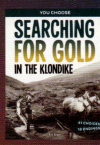

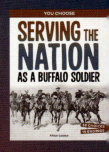

About the Author

Allison Lassieur loves to write books about real things, and she's very happy you've picked this book to read. She's written more than 150 nonfiction books about everything from medieval knights to the Loch Ness monster (okay, Nessie probably isn't real, but it was fun to write about her anyway). When she's not researching a book or writing one, Allison likes to read, knit, and eat chocolate cake. She lives in a very old house in upstate New York with her daughter, a sweet, silly dog, and more books than she can count.